Family Keepsake Journal

Mum,
I WANT TO
Hear Your Story®

A MOTHER'S GUIDED JOURNAL
TO SHARE HER LIFE & HER LOVE

"GOD COULD NOT BE EVERYWHERE & THEREFORE HE MADE MOTHERS."

– RUDYARD KIPLING

THIS BOOK HOLDS THE STORY OF

_____

_____

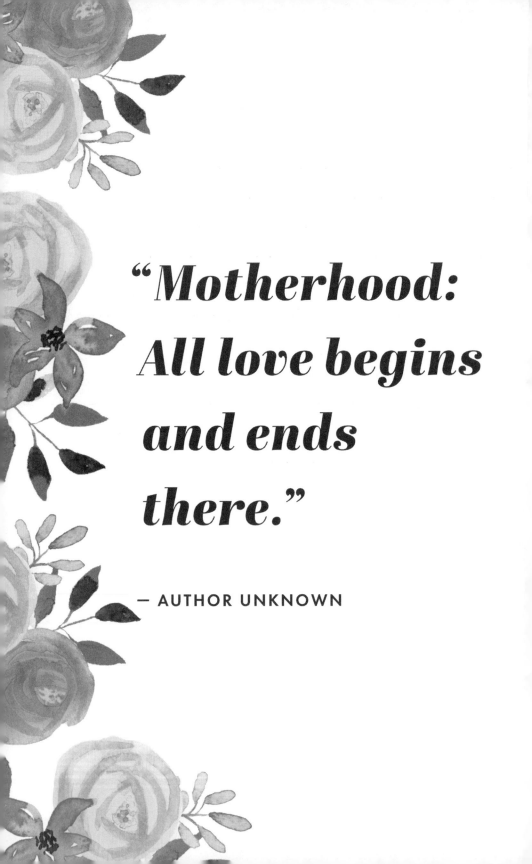

"**Motherhood:
All love begins
and ends
there.**"

— AUTHOR UNKNOWN

Table of Contents

Introduction

BECOMING A MOTHER MEANS choosing a life of sacrifice and devotion.

It means sharing your heartbeats with someone else and loving them without limits or endings.

Even after your children have grown and moved on, sleep remains a little less restful, your ears still listening for a midnight cry from a crib that hasn't been there for years.

Regardless of where life may take them, their joys, challenges and discoveries remain a part of your point and purpose.

Mum, I Want to Hear Your Story offers a place and a way for you to share your full life stories, allowing them to be learned, honoured and preserved.

It unveils your life beyond motherhood and shows your entire journey. It invites your loved ones to witness all you have experienced: every dream, every triumph, and every challenge.

Discovering your full life story allows our families to see more of how we are alike than different. With that comes understanding and connection.

This creates conversations, tightens bonds, and is a reminder of everything we give for and to our children.

"WHEN A CHILD
IS BORN,
THE MOTHER
IS BORN AGAIN."

– GILBERT PARKER

It's Your Birthday

What is your date of birth?

DAY	MONTH	YEAR

What time were you born?

_____ : _____ a.m. | p.m.

What was your full name at birth?

_____

_____

Were you named after a relative or someone else of significance?

_____

_____

If you had been given a vote, what name would you have picked for yourself?

_____

_____

In what city were you born?

_____

Were you born in a hospital? If not, where?

_____

_____

_____

What was your length and weight at birth?

_____

_____

How old were your parents when you were born?

_____

_____

Did your parents have any other children before you? If so, how old were your siblings when you were born?

_____

_____

_____

_____

What were your first words?

_____

_____

_____

How old were you when you started to walk?

_____

_____

_____

_____

What stories have you been told about the day you were born?

_____

_____

_____

_____

_____

_____

_____

_____

_____

How did your parents describe what you were like when you were a baby?

_____

_____

_____

_____

_____

_____

_____

_____

_____

What individuals cared for you the majority of the time when you were an infant?

_____

_____

_____

_____

_____

Are there any baby photos where you were dressed in outfits that you now find amusing? Describe a few.

_____

_____

_____

_____

_____

Do you know the titles of any books that were read to you when you were a baby?

_____

_____

_____

_____

_____

Was a lullaby or another song sung to help you go to sleep? If you know any of the words, write them below.

_____

_____

_____

_____

_____

_____

_____

_____

_____

_____

"Life began with waking up and loving my mother's face."

— GEORGE ELIOT

Google the following for the year you were born:

What were a few notable events that occurred that year?

_____

_____

_____

_____

_____

_____

_____

_____

What movie won the Academy Award for Best Picture?

_____

_____

Who won for Best Actor and Best Actress?

_____

_____

Which notable movies came out that year?

_____

_____

_____

_____

_____

What were a few popular songs that came out that year?

_____

_____

_____

_____

_____

_____

What were the most popular television shows?

_____

_____

_____

_____

_____

_____

_____

List the prices for the following items:

Loaf of bread: _____

Litre of milk: _____

Cup of tea: _____

A dozen eggs: _____

First class stamp: _____

Litre of petrol: _____

A cinema ticket: _____

The average cost of a new home: _____

"SOME DAYS
I WISH I COULD
GO BACK TO MY
CHILDHOOD.

NOT TO CHANGE
ANYTHING BUT
TO FEEL A FEW
THINGS TWICE."

– AUTHOR UNKNOWN

Childhood

What three words or phrases best describe your childhood?

_____

_____

_____

_____

_____

Describe what you were like when you were a kid.

_____

_____

_____

_____

_____

_____

_____

Did you have a nickname when you were growing up? What was it, and how did you get it?

_____

_____

_____

_____

_____

List the activities and sports you participated in.

_____

_____

_____

_____

_____

What music, dance, art or other lessons did you take? Did you enjoy them?

_____

_____

_____

_____

_____

What were your regular chores?

_____

_____

_____

_____

Did you receive an allowance? If yes, how much was it?

_____

_____

_____

_____

When you did have money, what did you typically spend it on?

_____

_____

_____

_____

_____

When you were a kid, what did you dream about becoming when you grew up?

_____

_____

_____

_____

_____

Who were your best friends during your primary school days? Are you still in contact with any of them?

_____

_____

_____

_____

_____

_____

What are a few movies you remember loving?

_____

_____

_____

_____

_____

_____

And what songs?

_____

_____

_____

_____

_____

Television shows?

_____

_____

_____

_____

_____

_____

What toys do you remember being especially attached to?

_____

_____

_____

_____

_____

_____

What books were a big part of your childhood?

_____

_____

_____

_____

_____

_____

Any games you remember playing a lot?

_____

_____

_____

_____

_____

_____

Was there a teacher or coach from your elementary school days that had a big influence on you?

_____

_____

_____

_____

_____

_____

What did they teach you, and what was their impact?

_____

_____

_____

_____

_____

_____

_____

_____

_____

_____

_____

_____

Did you have any pets when you were growing up? If yes, what were they, and what were their names?

_____

_____

_____

_____

_____

_____

_____

_____

What is a favourite memory of a childhood pet?

_____

_____

_____

_____

_____

_____

_____

_____

_____

What is a favourite childhood memory that fills you with nostalgia or happiness whenever it comes to mind?

If you could relive your childhood for one day, how would you choose to spend it?

_____

_____

_____

_____

_____

_____

_____

_____

_____

_____

"If you carry your childhood with you, you never become older."

— ABRAHAM SUTZKEVER

"A MOTHER IS SHE
WHO CAN TAKE
THE PLACE OF
ALL OTHERS BUT
WHOSE PLACE
NO ONE ELSE
CAN TAKE."

– CARDINAL MERMILLOD

The Teenage Years

What three words or phrases come to mind when you think back on your teenage years?

_____

_____

_____

_____

How would you describe yourself during this period of your life?

_____

_____

_____

_____

_____

_____

_____

_____

_____

_____

_____

_____

_____

How did you dress and style your hair during your secondary school years?

_____

_____

_____

_____

_____

Who were your closest friends during these years? When was the last time you spoke with any of them?

_____

_____

_____

_____

_____

_____

_____

_____

What were your parents' opinions on your choice in friends?

_____

_____

_____

_____

_____

Was there a group or activity that your social life and friend group tended to revolve around?

_____

_____

_____

_____

_____

_____

How did you spend a typical weekend night during your secondary school years?

_____

_____

_____

_____

_____

_____

Is there a specific place where you and your friends would hang out after school or on the weekends?

_____

_____

_____

_____

What was your curfew?

_____

_____

_____

_____

What is a memory of a time when you missed your curfew?

_____

_____

_____

_____

_____

_____

How did your parents respond to your being late?

_____

_____

_____

_____

Did you date during your secondary school years?

_____

_____

_____

_____

If yes, what was a typical date like for you in those years?

_____

_____

_____

_____

_____

_____

Did you go to any school dances?

_____

_____

_____

_____

_____

If yes, describe what they were like.

_____

_____

_____

_____

_____

_____

_____

_____

What activities or sports did you participate in during your teens?

_____

_____

_____

_____

_____

_____

Which of these were your favourites?

_____

_____

_____

_____

_____

_____

Which ones are interests or activities that are still a part of your life?

_____

_____

_____

_____

_____

_____

What year did you graduate from secondary school?

How many students were in your graduating class?

What were your favourite subjects in school?

And what were your least favourite?

What did you like the most about secondary school?

Did you ever skip school?

_____

_____

If yes, did you get away with it? What did you do during the time
you should have been in class?

_____

_____

_____

_____

What is something from secondary school or your teens that you
would like a chance to do over?

_____

_____

_____

_____

Were there any coming-of-age traditions that you participated
in during your teens or preteens (confirmation, bat mitzvah,
quinceañera, others)?

_____

_____

_____

_____

_____

_____

How did you spend your summers?

_____

_____

_____

_____

What jobs did you have during your secondary school years?

_____

_____

_____

Do you remember how much you were paid?

_____

_____

_____

"Today's tiny little moments become tomorrow's precious memories."

— AUTHOR UNKNOWN

What were a few of your favourite films?

_____

_____

_____

_____

_____

_____

And television shows?

_____

_____

_____

_____

_____

And books?

_____

_____

_____

_____

_____

What were your favourite kinds of music?

_____

_____

_____

_____

_____

Your favourite bands or recording artists?

_____

_____

_____

_____

_____

What were a few of your favourite songs?

_____

_____

_____

_____

_____

_____

_____

_____

_____

_____

_____

If you were to give it a name, what would you say was the overall theme of your bedroom?

_____

_____

What colour were the walls painted?

_____

_____

What did the bedding look like?

_____

_____

What did you have hanging on the walls?

_____

_____

_____

_____

Describe any additional details about how your teenage bedroom looked and felt.

_____

_____

_____

_____

_____

_____

_____

Looking back on this time, which moments and experiences stand out as transformative and defining?

_____

_____

_____

_____

_____

_____

_____

_____

_____

_____

_____

_____

_____

_____

_____

_____

_____

_____

_____

_____

_____

_____

What advice would you give your teenage self?

_____

_____

_____

_____

_____

_____

_____

_____

_____

_____

_____

_____

_____

_____

_____

_____

_____

_____

_____

_____

_____

What could the teenage version of you teach you today?

_____

_____

_____

_____

_____

_____

_____

_____

_____

_____

_____

_____

_____

_____

_____

_____

_____

_____

_____

_____

_____

_____

"ISN'T IT FUNNY HOW DAY BY DAY NOTHING CHANGES, BUT WHEN YOU LOOK BACK, EVERYTHING IS DIFFERENT?"

– C.S. LEWIS

Becoming an Adult

What did you do after secondary school? Did you serve in the armed forces, get a job or go to university, sixth form or a trade school? Something else?

_____

_____

_____

_____

_____

What were your reasons for making this choice?

_____

_____

_____

_____

_____

Looking back, how do you feel now about this decision?

_____

_____

_____

_____

_____

_____

How did this time period impact who you are today?

_____

_____

_____

_____

_____

_____

_____

If you could go back, what, if anything, would you change about this period of your life?

_____

_____

_____

_____

_____

_____

If you went to university or trade school, what did you study?

_____

_____

_____

_____

Describe what you were like in your twenties.

_____

_____

_____

_____

_____

What were your main goals and priorities during this time of your life?

_____

_____

_____

_____

_____

What advice would you give the twentysomething version of yourself?

_____

_____

_____

_____

_____

When you reflect on the person you were in your twenties and compare that to who you are today, what core parts of your identity or personality have stayed close to the same?

_____

_____

_____

_____

_____

_____

_____

_____

_____

_____

What has changed?

_____

_____

_____

_____

_____

_____

_____

_____

_____

_____

"Mothers hold their children's hands for a while but their hearts forever."

— AUTHOR UNKNOWN

Still reflecting back on your twenties, what pivotal choices or actions stand out as having had the most significant impact on the way your life moved forward?

_____

_____

_____

_____

_____

_____

_____

_____

What was your first major job after secondary school or university? How old were you? How much were you paid when you started?

_____

_____

_____

_____

Was there a job or profession your parents or family wanted you to pursue? What was it?

_____

_____

_____

_____

When people ask you what profession you are/were in, your response is...

_____

_____

_____

_____

How did you get into this career?

_____

_____

_____

_____

What are/were the best parts of this profession?

_____

_____

_____

_____

List a few of your work- and career-related achievements that you are proudest of.

_____

_____

_____

_____

_____

_____

Where is the first place you lived where you were the one who was responsible for paying the rent or mortgage? Do you remember the address?

_____

_____

_____

_____

How old were you when you moved there?

_____

Did you live on your own, or did you share the place?

_____

_____

What was your share of the rent/mortgage each month?

_____

_____

How long did you live there?

_____

_____

What was your favourite thing about this place?

_____

_____

_____

_____

_____

Describe the place. How many bedrooms and bathrooms did it have? What other things do you remember about it?

_____

_____

_____

_____

_____

_____

_____

_____

_____

What is a favourite memory from your time living there?

_____

_____

_____

_____

_____

_____

_____

_____

_____

_____

"LOVE DOESN'T
MAKE THE WORLD
GO 'ROUND.
LOVE IS WHAT
MAKES THE RIDE
WORTHWHILE."

– FRANKLIN P. JONES

Your Family

Think back to when you were growing up. What are three words or phrases that best describe your family?

_____

_____

_____

_____

How many nights each week on average would your family have dinner together?

_____

_____

_____

_____

When you did eat together, what was the typical routine for how the meal and the time together went?

_____

_____

_____

_____

_____

_____

_____

What did everyone usually talk about during the meal?

_____

_____

_____

_____

_____

Who did most of the cooking?

_____

_____

_____

_____

And who did most of the cleanup afterwards?

_____

_____

_____

_____

When you were a kid, what were a few of your favourite things that were served for dinner?

_____

_____

_____

_____

_____

And what were the dishes that would make you grimace?

_____

_____

What would happen if you wouldn't eat something?

_____

_____

What holiday was the biggest event for your family when you were growing up?

_____

_____

What were some of the most memorable ways your family would observe this holiday?

_____

_____

_____

_____

_____

_____

_____

How were birthdays, anniversaries and individual achievements commemorated by your family?

_____

_____

_____

_____

_____

_____

Did your family set aside regular quality time together (things like movie nights or game nights)? If so, what did you do together?

_____

_____

_____

_____

_____

_____

Did you have any relatives who lived nearby who were a big part of your family life?

_____

_____

_____

_____

_____

_____

What role did they have in how you were raised?

_____

_____

_____

_____

_____

_____

_____

What values, beliefs and rules were strongly emphasised during your upbringing?

_____

_____

_____

_____

_____

_____

_____

_____

_____

_____

_____

_____

_____

What were the expectations and requirements in areas such as grades, chores and participation in extracurricular activities or sports?

In what ways does the family environment you created for your children compare to the one you grew up in?

_____

_____

_____

_____

_____

_____

_____

_____

_____

Was there anything you consciously did differently?

_____

_____

_____

_____

_____

_____

_____

_____

_____

Time can create changes in perspective. Looking back, how have your views on your upbringing and coming-of-age years changed over time?

_____

_____

_____

_____

_____

_____

_____

_____

_____

_____

_____

_____

_____

_____

_____

_____

_____

_____

_____

"*Life isn't about finding yourself.*

Life is about creating yourself."

— GEORGE BERNARD SHAW

What is a favourite memory you have of a time you spent with your family during your childhood?

_____

_____

_____

_____

_____

_____

_____

_____

_____

_____

_____

_____

_____

_____

_____

_____

_____

_____

_____

_____

What is a favourite memory you have of a time you spent with your family as an adult?

_____

_____

_____

_____

_____

_____

_____

_____

_____

_____

_____

_____

_____

_____

_____

_____

_____

_____

_____

_____

Your Family Tree

_____

MY GREAT-GRANDFATHER

(My Grandfather's Dad)

_____

MY GREAT-GRANDMOTHER

(My Grandfather's Mum)

_____

MY GREAT-GRANDFATHER

(My Grandmother's Dad)

_____

MY GREAT-GRANDMOTHER

(My Grandmother's Mum)

_____

MY GRANDFATHER

(My Dad's Dad)

_____

MY GRANDMOTHER

(My Dad's Mum)

_____

MY FATHER

_____

MY GREAT-GRANDFATHER

(My Grandfather's Dad)

_____

MY GREAT-GRANDMOTHER

(My Grandfather's Mum)

_____

MY GREAT-GRANDFATHER

(My Grandmother's Dad)

_____

MY GREAT-GRANDMOTHER

(My Grandmother's Mum)

_____

MY GRANDFATHER

(My Mum's Dad)

_____

MY GRANDMOTHER

(My Mum's Mum)

_____

MY MOTHER

"FAMILIES ARE LIKE BRANCHES ON A TREE. WE GROW IN DIFFERENT DIRECTIONS, YET OUR ROOTS REMAIN AS ONE."

– AUTHOR UNKNOWN

Parents & Grandparents

What was your mother's full name?

_____

Where was she born?

_____

Where did she grow up?

_____

_____

_____

_____

_____

What was your father's full name?

_____

Where was he born?

_____

Where did he grow up?

_____

_____

_____

_____

_____

What three words or phrases best describe your mother?

_____

_____

_____

_____

_____

In what ways are you most like her?

_____

_____

_____

_____

_____

_____

_____

_____

Reflect on and share the qualities and values you most admire in your mother.

_____

_____

_____

_____

_____

_____

What three words or phrases best describe your father?

_____

_____

_____

_____

_____

In what ways are you most like him?

_____

_____

_____

_____

_____

_____

_____

Reflect on and share the qualities and values you most admire in your father.

_____

_____

_____

_____

_____

_____

_____

What was your mother's maiden name?

_____

_____

From what part(s) of the world did your mother's family originate?

_____

_____

_____

What was your father's mother's maiden name?

_____

_____

From what part(s) of the world did your father's family originate?

_____

_____

_____

How did your parents meet?

_____

_____

_____

_____

_____

_____

_____

What were their ages when they first met?

_____

_____

When and where were they married? How old was each at the time?

_____

_____

_____

What stories have you been told about their wedding day?

_____

_____

_____

_____

_____

_____

_____

_____

_____

_____

_____

_____

_____

_____

List a few of their hobbies, interests, talents and skills.

_____

_____

_____

_____

_____

What were their educational backgrounds?

_____

_____

_____

_____

What were your parents' professions?

_____

_____

_____

_____

Did either of them serve in the armed forces?

_____

_____

_____

_____

Parents will often repeat certain words of wisdom, sayings and proverbs when giving advice to their kids. What are a few you often heard growing up?

Write about a favourite memory of your mother.

_____

_____

_____

_____

_____

_____

_____

_____

_____

_____

_____

_____

_____

_____

_____

_____

_____

_____

_____

_____

_____

_____

"Motherhood is the only job that matters."

— QUEEN ELIZABETH II

Write about a favourite memory of your father.

What were the names of your grandparents on your mother's side of your family?

_____

_____

What was your maternal grandmother's maiden name?

_____

What did you call your maternal grandparents?

_____

_____

Where were they born, and where did they grow up?

_____

_____

_____

_____

What was their highest level of education?

_____

_____

_____

_____

What were their professions?

_____

_____

_____

_____

Describe what they were like.

_____

_____

_____

_____

_____

_____

_____

_____

_____

_____

_____

_____

_____

_____

_____

_____

_____

_____

_____

_____

_____

_____

_____

_____

What is a favourite memory of your grandparents on your mum's side?

_____

_____

_____

_____

_____

_____

_____

_____

_____

_____

What were the names of your grandparents on your father's side of your family?

_____

_____

What was your paternal grandmother's maiden name?

_____

What did you call your paternal grandparents?

_____

_____

_____

Where were they born, and where did they grow up?

_____

_____

_____

_____

What was their highest level of education?

_____

_____

_____

_____

What were their professions?

_____

_____

_____

_____

What is a favourite memory of your grandparents on your father's side?

_____

_____

_____

_____

_____

_____

_____

Describe what they were like.

_____

_____

_____

_____

_____

_____

_____

_____

_____

_____

_____

_____

_____

_____

_____

_____

_____

_____

_____

_____

_____

_____

Did you ever meet your great-grandparents on either side of your family? If yes, what were they like?

_____

_____

_____

_____

_____

_____

_____

_____

_____

_____

_____

_____

_____

_____

_____

_____

_____

_____

_____

_____

_____

What other individuals had a major role in helping you grow up?
What was each one's contribution to who you have become?

_____

_____

_____

_____

_____

_____

_____

_____

_____

_____

_____

_____

_____

_____

_____

_____

_____

_____

_____

_____

"THERE ARE
TWO GIFTS
WE GIVE OUR
CHILDREN.
ONE IS ROOTS,
THE OTHER
IS WINGS."

– AUTHOR UNKNOWN

Your Siblings

Are you an only child, or do you have siblings?

_____

_____

Where are you in the birth order?

_____

_____

List your siblings' names in order of their ages. Be sure to include yourself.

_____

_____

_____

_____

_____

_____

Do you feel things were easier or harder for you when you were growing up because of where you fell in the birth order? Why?

_____

_____

_____

_____

Which of your siblings were you the closest with when you were young?

_____

_____

_____

Which of your siblings have you been the closest with during your adult years?

_____

_____

_____

Did you look up to any of them when you were growing up?

_____

_____

_____

If yes, write about a time when you did something to impress them or be like them.

_____

_____

_____

_____

_____

_____

_____

_____

What is something you admire about each of your siblings?

_____

_____

_____

_____

_____

_____

_____

_____

_____

_____

_____

_____

_____

_____

_____

_____

_____

_____

_____

_____

_____

Did you share a bedroom with any of them?

_____

_____

_____

_____

_____

If yes, what are your memories of the experience?

_____

_____

_____

_____

_____

What is the best part about having a sibling?

_____

_____

_____

_____

_____

_____

_____

_____

_____

Write about a favourite memory from your childhood that shows the bond you shared with your siblings.

_____

_____

_____

_____

_____

_____

_____

_____

_____

_____

_____

_____

_____

_____

_____

_____

_____

_____

_____

"BEING A MOTHER MEANS THAT YOUR HEART IS NO LONGER YOURS; IT WANDERS WHEREVER YOUR CHILDREN DO."

– GEORGE BERNARD SHAW

Becoming a Mum

How old were you when you first became a mother?

_____

Think back to the moment when you found out you were pregnant with your first child. Do you remember your first reaction or the first thing you said?

_____

_____

_____

What were your initial thoughts, feelings and emotions?

_____

_____

_____

_____

Who was the first person you told?

_____

_____

_____

What was their reaction?

_____

_____

_____

Write about the first time you saw your baby on a sonogram or heard their heartbeat. Be sure to include your reactions, feelings and emotions.

_____

_____

_____

_____

_____

Describe the first time you felt your baby move or kick.

_____

_____

_____

_____

What are some of the more memorable food cravings you had during your pregnancies?

_____

_____

_____

_____

_____

Write about a particularly sentimental, surprising or humorous moment from each of your pregnancies.

What was your favourite part about being pregnant?

_____

_____

_____

_____

_____

_____

_____

What was the process for selecting your children's names?

_____

_____

_____

_____

_____

_____

Were there any disagreements or negotiations over any of the names?

_____

_____

_____

_____

_____

What is the inspiration for each of your children's names?

_____

_____

_____

_____

_____

_____

_____

What was the biggest surprise about being a mum that you discovered after your first child arrived?

_____

_____

_____

_____

_____

_____

_____

_____

_____

_____

_____

_____

What were your children's lengths and weights at birth?

_____

_____

_____

_____

_____

How old were they when they took their first steps?

_____

_____

_____

_____

_____

What were their first words?

_____

_____

_____

_____

_____

Is there a special song you would sing or play for your children when they were little?

_____

_____

_____

_____

What tricks would you use to help them relax or fall asleep?

_____

_____

_____

_____

_____

_____

_____

Are there any specific books you remember reading to your children?

_____

_____

_____

_____

_____

_____

_____

How did motherhood impact your professional life?

_____

_____

_____

_____

_____

_____

_____

What are the best parts of being a mother?

_____

_____

_____

_____

_____

_____

_____

_____

_____

Write about something profound or unexpected you have learned about life from being a mother and having children.

_____

_____

_____

_____

_____

_____

_____

_____

_____

_____

What advice would you go back and give yourself when you were a new mother?

_____

_____

_____

_____

_____

_____

_____

_____

_____

_____

"**Life doesn't come
with a manual;
it comes with a mother.**"

— AUTHOR UNKNOWN

Write about how being a mother and having children have transformed or magnified your definition of what love is.

_____

_____

_____

_____

_____

_____

_____

_____

_____

How has being a mom and raising children shaped or reshaped your perspective and understanding of your own mother or parents?

_____

_____

_____

_____

_____

_____

_____

_____

_____

When you reflect on your life before and after having children, what are the significant ways becoming and being a mother has changed you?

_____

_____

_____

_____

_____

_____

_____

_____

_____

_____

_____

_____

_____

_____

_____

_____

_____

_____

_____

_____

"WHAT WE HAVE
ONCE ENJOYED WE
CAN NEVER LOSE.

ALL THAT WE
LOVE DEEPLY
BECOMES
A PART OF US."

– HELEN KELLER

Love & Romance

Do you believe in love at first sight?

_____

_____

Do you believe in soulmates?

_____

_____

What age were you when you went on your first date?

_____

_____

Can you remember who it was with and what you did?

_____

_____

_____

_____

_____

How old were you when you had your first steady relationship?
Who was it with?

_____

_____

_____

_____

Were you ever in a relationship with someone your parents did not approve of?

_____

_____

_____

_____

Did you have any celebrity crushes when you were young? Who were the most memorable?

_____

_____

_____

_____

When you were younger, did you have a type you were attracted to? Describe it.

_____

_____

_____

_____

How did you meet our dad?

_____

_____

_____

_____

_____

How did he ask you out for your first date (or did you ask him)?

_____

_____

_____

_____

_____

_____

What did you do on your first date?

_____

_____

_____

_____

_____

_____

_____

What were your impressions and thoughts about him after that first date?

_____

_____

_____

_____

_____

_____

_____

Do you remember the first time you thought that he might be "the one"? What was it about him, or what did he do to help you to feel this way?

_____

_____

_____

_____

_____

_____

How long did you date before you became engaged?

_____

_____

What is the story of your proposal?

_____

_____

_____

_____

_____

_____

_____

_____

_____

Who as the first person you told that you were engaged?

_____

_____

_____

Describe their reaction.

_____

_____

_____

_____

_____

How much time was there between when you became engaged and the actual wedding date?

_____

What was the process for planning the wedding like? Who did most of the work? Were there any challenges?

_____

_____

_____

_____

_____

_____

_____

Did either of you have a hen or stag party? If yes, where was it held?

_____

_____

_____

_____

_____

_____

Where was the wedding held?

_____

_____

_____

How about the reception?

_____

_____

_____

How many people were invited to the wedding?

_____

_____

_____

And how many people attended?

_____

_____

_____

Who were the best man and maid of honor?

_____

_____

And the groomsmen?

_____

_____

_____

_____

_____

_____

And the bridesmaids?

_____

_____

_____

_____

_____

_____

_____

Any other members of the wedding party?

_____

_____

_____

_____

_____

_____

_____

_____

_____

_____

_____

_____

_____

_____

_____

_____

_____

_____

What was your wedding like, and who was there? Any good wedding day stories?

_____

_____

_____

_____

_____

_____

_____

_____

_____

_____

_____

_____

_____

_____

_____

_____

_____

_____

_____

_____

_____

What moment from your entire wedding day do you remember the most vividly?

_____

_____

_____

_____

_____

Did you have a honeymoon? If yes, where did you go?

_____

_____

_____

_____

_____

What advice would you want to go back and give yourself the morning of your wedding day?

_____

_____

_____

_____

_____

_____

This is room to write about any other memories of getting married or additional weddings you may have had.

_____

_____

_____

_____

_____

_____

_____

_____

_____

_____

_____

_____

_____

_____

_____

_____

_____

_____

_____

_____

_____

"LIFE CAN
ONLY BE
UNDERSTOOD
BACKWARDS,
BUT IT MUST BE
LIVED FORWARDS."

– SOREN KIERKEGAARD

Favourites, Thoughts & Advice

If you were to write your autobiography, what title would you select to convey and describe your life story?

_____

_____

_____

_____

What is a favourite quote, scripture or prayer?

_____

_____

_____

_____

_____

What superpower would you choose for yourself?

_____

_____

_____

What is your biggest fear?

_____

_____

_____

_____

If you could live anywhere in the world for a year with all expenses paid, where would you choose?

_____

_____

_____

_____

_____

What is a travel experience that changed your opinions and perspective about a part of the country or the larger world?

_____

_____

_____

_____

_____

_____

_____

_____

What is a favourite memory of a meal you had while traveling?

_____

_____

_____

_____

What is a favourite travel memory?

_____

_____

_____

_____

_____

_____

_____

_____

_____

_____

_____

_____

_____

_____

_____

_____

_____

_____

_____

_____

_____

_____

_____

List your ten favourite destinations you have travelled to.

1. _____

   _____

2. _____

   _____

3. _____

   _____

4. _____

   _____

5. _____

   _____

6. _____

   _____

7. _____

   _____

8. _____

   _____

9. _____

   _____

10. _____

   _____

List the top ten places you would visit if money and time were no concern.

1. _____

   _____

2. _____

   _____

3. _____

   _____

4. _____

   _____

5. _____

   _____

6. _____

   _____

7. _____

   _____

8. _____

   _____

9. _____

   _____

10. _____

    _____

What song would you pick as the theme song of your life?

_____

_____

_____

_____

_____

In your opinion, which decades had the best music?

_____

_____

_____

_____

_____

What is a song from your teens that reminds you of a special event or moment from that time? Write about that memory.

_____

_____

_____

_____

_____

_____

_____

_____

_____

How has your taste in music changed over the years?

_____

_____

_____

_____

What is the first record (or album, cassette, CD, etc.) you can remember buying or receiving as a gift?

_____

_____

_____

_____

What was the first concert you attended? Where was it held and when? What do you remember about it?

_____

_____

_____

_____

_____

_____

_____

_____

_____

_____

What are your ten favourite songs of all time?

1. _____

_____

2. _____

_____

3. _____

_____

4. _____

_____

5. _____

_____

6. _____

_____

7. _____

_____

8. _____

_____

9. _____

_____

10. _____

_____

What are a few movies from your childhood and teens that you still enjoy watching?

_____

_____

_____

_____

_____

_____

_____

If you were going to make a movie about your life, what would the title be?

_____

_____

_____

_____

What genre would the movie be (rom-com, thriller, science fiction, drama, etc.)?

_____

_____

_____

_____

_____

Who would you cast to play you?

_____

_____

_____

How about the rest of your family?

_____

_____

_____

_____

_____

_____

_____

_____

What are a few television shows and films that are a must-watch around the holidays?

_____

_____

_____

_____

_____

_____

_____

What are ten of your most favourite films?

1. _____

   _____

2. _____

   _____

3. _____

   _____

4. _____

   _____

5. _____

   _____

6. _____

   _____

7. _____

   _____

8. _____

   _____

9. _____

   _____

10. _____

   _____

What television show from the past do you wish was still making new episodes?

_____

_____

_____

How many books would you say you read each year? How many have you read in your lifetime?

_____

_____

_____

When you do read, what are your favourite genres?

_____

_____

_____

_____

_____

Who are some of your favourite authors?

_____

_____

_____

_____

_____

_____

_____

What book or books have majorly impacted the way you think, work or live your life?

What is a favourite memory from the last twelve months?

_____

_____

_____

_____

_____

_____

_____

_____

_____

What in your life has brought you the greatest joy and contentment?

_____

_____

_____

_____

_____

_____

_____

_____

_____

What are a few personal accomplishments you are especially proud of?

_____

_____

_____

_____

_____

_____

_____

_____

Which has the most impact on our lives: fate or free will?

_____

_____

_____

_____

What do you believe is the purpose of our lives?

_____

_____

_____

_____

_____

How did you define success for yourself when you were younger?

_____

_____

_____

_____

_____

_____

_____

_____

_____

How do you define success for yourself now?

_____

_____

_____

_____

_____

_____

_____

_____

_____

_____

What role did religion have in your family when you were growing up?

_____

_____

_____

_____

_____

_____

_____

_____

_____

Were there any specific religious rituals, celebrations or traditions that your family observed?

_____

_____

_____

_____

_____

_____

_____

_____

_____

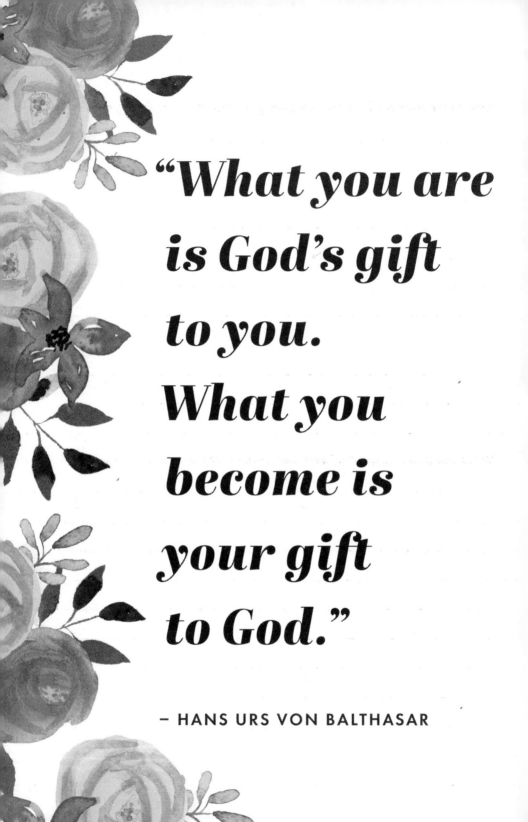

"What you are is God's gift to you. What you become is your gift to God."

– HANS URS VON BALTHASAR

How have your spiritual beliefs changed over the course of your life?

_____

_____

_____

_____

_____

_____

_____

_____

_____

What religious or spiritual practices are currently a part of your life?

_____

_____

_____

_____

_____

_____

_____

_____

_____

_____

_____

Which individuals do you feel especially grateful to for the role they played in your life story? Be sure to describe how each one has impacted you.

_____

_____

_____

_____

_____

_____

_____

_____

_____

_____

_____

_____

_____

_____

_____

_____

_____

_____

_____

_____

FAVOURITES, THOUGHTS & ADVICE

When you look back over the course of your life, what events and experiences had the biggest impact in shaping the person you are today?

_____

_____

_____

_____

_____

_____

_____

_____

_____

_____

_____

_____

_____

_____

_____

_____

_____

_____

_____

_____

FAVOURITES, THOUGHTS & ADVICE

When you think over the ups and downs of your life, what was a time that stands out as especially spiritually or emotionally demanding?

_____

_____

_____

_____

_____

_____

_____

What do you do when times are challenging, and you need to find additional inner strength and perseverance?

_____

_____

_____

_____

_____

_____

_____

What advice on how to live one's best life would you offer to someone in their twenties and thirties?

_____

_____

_____

_____

_____

_____

_____

_____

_____

And what lessons about life do you think you could learn from someone in their twenties or thirties?

_____

_____

_____

_____

_____

_____

_____

_____

_____

The following pages are for you to expand on some of your answers, share more memories and/or write notes to your loved ones.

_____

_____

_____

_____

_____

_____

_____

_____

_____

_____

_____

_____

_____

_____

_____

_____

_____

_____

_____

_____

_____

_____

FAVOURITES, THOUGHTS & ADVICE

FAVOURITES, THOUGHTS & ADVICE

FAVOURITES, THOUGHTS & ADVICE

FAVOURITES, THOUGHTS & ADVICE

_____

_____

_____

_____

_____

_____

_____

_____

_____

_____

_____

_____

_____

_____

_____

_____

_____

_____

_____

_____

_____

_____

_____

_____

_____

FAVOURITES, THOUGHTS & ADVICE

HEAR YOUR STORY
Books & Guided Journals

AT HEAR YOUR STORY, we have created a line of books focused on giving each of us a place to tell the unique story of who we are, where we have been, and where we are going.

Sharing and hearing the stories of the people in our life creates a closeness and understanding, ultimately strengthening our bonds.

Mom, I Want to Hear Your Story:
A Mother's Guided Journal to Share Her Life and Her Love

Dad, I Want to Hear Your Story:
A Father's Guided Journal to Share His Life and His Love

Grandmother, I Want to Hear Your Story:
A Grandmother's Guided Journal to Share Her Life and Her Love

Grandfather, I Want to Hear Your Story:
A Grandfather's Guided Journal to Share His Life and His Love

Tell Your Life Story:
The Write-Your-Own-Autobiography Guided Journal

To My Wonderful Aunt, I Want to Hear Your Story:
A Guided Journal to Share Her Life and Her Love

To My Uncle, I Want to Hear Your Story:
A Guided Journal to Share His Life and His Love

Mom & Me: Let's Learn Together Journal for Kids

Mom, I Want to Learn Your Recipes
A Keepsake Family Memory Cookbook

Grandmother, I Want to Learn Your Recipes
A Keepsake Family Memory Cookbook

Dad, I Want to Learn Your Recipes
A Keepsake Family Memory Cookbook

Grandfather, I Want to Learn Your Recipes
A Keepsake Family Memory Cookbook

Aunt, I Want to Learn Your Recipes
A Keepsake Family Memory Cookbook

Uncle, I Want to Learn Your Recipes
A Keepsake Family Memory Cookbook

Sibling, I Want to Learn Your Recipes
A Keepsake Family Memory Cookbook

Friend, I Want to Learn Your Recipes
A Keepsake Family Memory Cookbook

FIND MORE FAMILY
CONNECTION AT
@hearyourstorybooks
hearyourstorybooks.com

About Hear Your Story

AT HEAR YOUR STORY®, we're dedicated to capturing and cherishing life's priceless moments. We passionately believe that within everyone is a treasure of memories and stories that need to be told, cherished and passed on through generations.

Our journey began from a deeply personal heartache for our founder: watching Alzheimer's steal his father's creativity, curiosity and memories. From that pain emerged a profound realisation—the importance of preserving every precious life story.

Hear Your Story offers more than a beautifully designed journal. We provide a bridge to the past, guiding you or your loved one through cherished memories. It's a gift of reflection, connection and legacy.

Envision you and your family sitting together as your loved one's journal is shared, smiles everywhere, conversations sparked and connections deepened. In an age where moments can easily fade, Hear Your Story offers something tangible, lasting—a treasured heirloom of life's adventures.

Join us, and let's celebrate every tale. At Hear Your Story, we turn memories into heirlooms.

Published by Hear Your Story, an imprint of Sourcebooks
P.O. Box 4410, Naperville, Illinois 60567-4410
(630) 961-3900
sourcebooks.com

Originally published as *Mum, I Want to Hear Your Story* in 2019
in the United States of America by EYP Publishing, LLC.

Printed and bound in the United Kingdom.
CPI 10 9 8 7 6 5 4 3 2 1